Volcano Alert!

Written by Caitlin Fraser

Illustrated by Naomi Lewis

Flying Start
to Literacy®

T0363490

Contents

Chapter 1: Eruption alert!

Ivan and Demi were working on Mount Fulton, an active volcano. It was their job to collect information about the volcano, which they knew was likely to erupt at any time.

Suddenly they heard an explosion. Smoke began billowing out of cracks in the mountain.

Demi looked worried.
"I think we should leave now," she said.
"It's too dangerous to stay any longer."

"We have to send out an alert to the town," said Ivan as they ran. Soon the hot lava from the volcano would be flowing down the mountain.

Ivan spoke into his radio. "Mount Fulton is beginning to erupt! Tell everyone to get out of town. NOW!"

Chapter 2: Evacuate!

When Ivan and Demi reached the town, people were leaving.

Demi and Ivan looked at the volcano. More and more smoke and ash were coming out of it.

"There is a big problem," said Demi looking at her computer.

"It looks like the lava is going to flow over the town," said Demi.

"The lava will burn everything in its path," said Ivan. "How can we stop the lava from flowing over the town?"

"A wall of rocks near the river could protect the town. It might make the lava flow away from the town," said Demi.

"Great idea," said Ivan. "We'll need lots of people to help us. But we only have a short time before the lava reaches the town."

Chapter 3:
A town under threat

Everyone worked as quickly as they could to make the wall of rocks near the river.

They drove trucks filled with gravel and rocks to the river.

They used bulldozers to push the gravel and rocks into piles along the side of the river.

They used shovels to
pack dirt around the rocks
to make the wall strong.

As they worked, loud explosions
from the mountain made the
ground tremble, and smoke filled
the air.

The rock wall got bigger and bigger,
and the sky got darker and darker.
The air was thick with smoke and ash.

"It's not safe here anymore," said Ivan.
"We all need to leave ... and quickly."

"Will the wall stop the lava from
flowing into the town?" asked Demi.

"I don't know," said Ivan.
"It's never been done before."

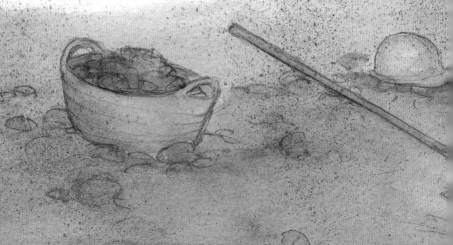

Chapter 4:
A river of fire

As Ivan and Demi drove away,
they heard a huge explosion.
One side of the mountain
had been blown away!

Gas, ash, pieces of rock and steam
spewed out of the volcano. Lava
flowed down the side of the mountain.
It was heading straight for the town.
It looked like a river of fire and
it burned everything in its path.

Demi and Ivan watched as the lava reached the rock wall. It began creeping up the sides of the wall, getting closer and closer to the top. Ivan and Demi held their breath.

Then just when it seemed that the lava would flow over the top of the rock wall and into the town, it started to flow in another direction.
The wall had worked.

Chapter 5:
A lucky save

When the eruption was over,
everyone came back to
the town.

Demi and Ivan had
saved the town.

A note from the author

I once read about a town that had built a wall out of rock and earth to protect itself when Mount Etna erupted. It was the first time this had been attempted and no one knew if it would work. Luckily, it was successful and the town was saved.

I imagined how hard the people must have worked to build this barrier and what a frightening time it must have been for those who lived in the area. And that is how the idea for *Volcano Alert!* was born.